my trip
to
Gettysburg

PELICAN PUBLISHING COMPANY
Gretna 2007

Author: J. Patrick Polley
Photographs: J. Patrick Polley, PhotoDisc©, Library of Congress
Illustrations: Kevin R. Hanstick
Design: Infinite Ideas & Designs
Copyright© 2007 Vinings Publishing
All rights reserved
ISBN-13: 978-1-58980-456-2

Printed in Malaysia
Published by Pelican Publishing Company, Inc.
1000 Burmaster Street, Gretna, Louisiana 70053

*After two years of bloody warfare, the Union
and Confederate armies had both scored victories
and suffered defeats. Anxious to take the war
to the North in order to obtain supplies, and
perhaps even British and French recognition
of the Confederacy as an independent nation,
Robert E. Lee led the Army of Northern Virginia
in an invasion in June of 1862. The Army of
the Potomac, first under the command of Joseph
Hooker then later Gordon Meade, followed close
behind. The two armies collided in a three-day
battle on the low hills and ridges around the small
Pennsylvania town of Gettysburg on July 1-3,
1863. The two armies suffered nearly 50,000
casualties, and Lee's invasion was turned back.*

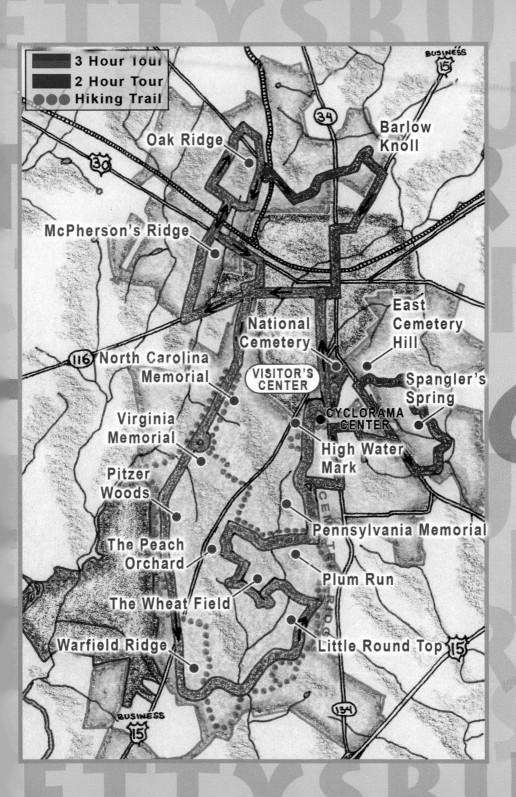

3 Hour Tour
2 Hour Tour
Hiking Trail

Oak Ridge

Barlow Knoll

McPherson's Ridge

National Cemetery

East Cemetery Hill

VISITOR'S CENTER

North Carolina Memorial

Spangler's Spring

CYCLORAMA CENTER

Virginia Memorial

High Water Mark

Pitzer Woods

Pennsylvania Memorial

The Peach Orchard

Plum Run

The Wheat Field

Warfield Ridge

Little Round Top

BUSINESS 15

CENTER RIDGE

The First Day of My Trip

Date I am visiting

How I arrived

People with me

Important things I want to see

What I hope to learn

Use this page
record all ki
of import
informat
about your t

McPherson's Ridge

Day I visited

Who I was with

The first thing I noticed was

Any battles here would have been extremely

fierce because

The monument says

The most important thing I learned here

Pull off into one of the marked turnoffs and you can look back along McPherson's Ridge. The Union I Corps had its main defensive line here during the early fighting on the first day of the battle, July 1. You'll notice the ridge isn't very high, but from the top of it you can see the surrounding terrain well. This high ground gave the Union troops excellent fields of fire when defending against the Confederate attacks here.

NEW YORK

You'll see many monuments as you tour the battlefield. The statue on the pedestal is General Abner Doubleday. He commanded the 1st Division of the Union I Corps, but is more famous as the legendary inventor of the game of baseball.

The large stone cross is a Union regimental marker to the 142nd Pennsylvania Infantry Regiment. This monument was erected in 1889. During the 3 days of the battle the regiment suffered the loss of 211 enlisted men and officers out of a total of 336.

Day I visited

Who I was with

The first thing I noticed was

The monuments teach me that

The Union regimental marker made me feel

One thing I'll remember is

Day I visited

Who I was with

The first thing I noticed was

This statue taught me that

The cannon barrels are

The neatest thing was

As you continue on Reynolds Avenue you cross Chambersburg Pike and make a left to visit a piece of the battlefield not covered by the National Park Service Auto Tour. On the right-hand side of Chambersburg Pike you'll see a statue standing atop a monument with four cannon barrels around it. The man on the pedestal is General John Buford, who commanded the Union cavalry that made first contact with the Confederates. The cannon barrels are from the Union artillery battery that fired the first Union artillery shots of the battle.

8th New York Cavalry Regiment

Look at the cavalryman on his horse. He has a saber by his side, but is carrying his carbine, a short rifle. The breech-loading carbines carried by the Union cavalry could be fired twice as quickly as a muzzle-loading rifle. The fire from the cavalry carbines was a big factor in holding off the Confederate infantry until the Union I Corps arrived later in the morning.

You'll also see an inscription on the monument underneath the trooper. "Discovering the Enemy" was one of the primary tasks of cavalry. Cavalry was used to find out where and how strong enemy units were. The absence of the Confederate cavalry for much of the battle led to the Confederate army operating with limited information of the Union forces and dispositions.

Date I visited

Who I was with

The first thing I noticed was

One thing I learned about the cavalry is

If the Confederate army had used a cavalry then how might things have been different?

MAD LIB

MAD LIB

Before looking at the story below, write in what words come to mind in the columns below. Then fill in the blank spaces with the words you have picked according to the number.

1. Adjective _____
2. Person's Name _____
3. Verb _____
4. Verb _____
5. Noun _____
6. Adjective _____
7. Animal _____
8. Verb ending in "ing" _____
9. Verb _____
10. Adjective _____
11. Person's Name _____
12. Adjective _____

13. Verb _____
14. Adverb _____
15. Adjective _____
16. Plural noun _____
17. Adjective _____
18. Plural Noun _____
19. Verb _____
20. Plural Noun _____
21. Two Digit Number _____
22. Verb _____
23. Adverb _____
24. Verb _____

Dear Diary,

I can't believe I'm visiting 1. _____ Gettysburg. This morning I thought

2. _____ would 3. _____ three cows when I said I wanted to

4. _____ while I visited today. The first thing I want to see is a 5. _____

because I've always wondered what a/an 6. _____ 7. _____ really

looked like. Then, after 8. _____ lunch, I want to 9. _____ in the 10.

_____ field. 11._____ says that I must be 12. _____ if I think I

can 13. _____ by myself. But that's okay, because I know that once I

14. _____ see the monuments, I will have learned a lot about 15. _____

___ 16. _____ and 17. _____ 18. _____. I think that I also

want to 19._____ 20._____ when I get there. That way I will learn

21._____ ways to 22. _____ in a battle, so I ever have to fight in a war,

I will 23. _____ 24. _____.

John Burns, born in 1794 and a veteran of the War of 1812, was the only and oldest civilian known to have fought alongside the Union forces at Gettysburg. This statue memorializes him and his service on July 1, and was dedicated on the 40th anniversary of the battle, on July 1, 1903. At the age of 70, Burns fought first in the ranks of the 150th Pennsylvania Infantry, then with the Iron Brigade. He was wounded three times, but recovered. After the war, he received a personal thanks from Abraham Lincoln. He died in 1872, and is buried in Evergreen Cemetery on Cemetery Hill.

Day that I visited

Who I was with

The first thing I noticed was

When I learned that John Burns was 70 I felt

The statue made me feel

Flank Markers

Date that I visited _____

Who I was with _____

_____

The first thing I noticed was _____

_____

_____

_____

_____

_____

The markers were/weren't interesting because _____

_____

_____

_____

_____

One interesting thing I learned was _____

_____

_____

_____

_____

_____

You'll see many of these low square markers as you tour the battlefield. The markers indicate the positions of the ends of a regimental line during an important point in the battle. The markers have an "L" or "R" on them to mark the left or right flank of the regiment. Sometimes the "left" or "right" is spelled out as in the picture.

The two markers are for the right flank of the 2nd Wisconsin Volunteer Infantry (W.V.I.) and the 7th Wisconsin Volunteer Infantry, which were two of the five infantry regiments that made up the famous Iron Brigade in the 1st Division of the I Corps.

The marker shown in the picture is for a Confederate infantry brigade commanded by General Archer during July 1. This brigade attacked Union positions on McPherson's Ridge but was driven back by the Iron Brigade during the morning of July1.

During the repulse of his brigade, General Archer was captured. As he was being led to the rear, General Doubleday met him. The two generals, now on opposite sides, had known each other in the army before the war. General Doubleday, showing more good feeling than tact, extended his hand and exclaimed that he was glad to see his old friend. Archer refused to shake hands, replying that he sure wasn't glad to see Doubleday. Being a prisoner of war tends to make generals prickly.

Day that I visited

Who I was with

The first thing I noticed was

One reason the Union was able to drive the Confederates back here from McPherson's Ridge might have been

This marker tells me that

Regimental Markers

Day I visited

Who I was with

The first thing I noticed was

These markers pay tribute to

The most interesting thing I learned here is

As you turn down along Meredith Drive you pass three regimental markers dedicated to three of the five regiments that made up the famous Iron Brigade. The monuments here commemorate the 2nd Wisconsin, 7th Wisconsin, and 24th Michigan Infantry Regiments. The small square stone monument shown on this page is dedicated to the 24th Michigan. On July 1, the 24th Michigan went into action with 496 men. At the conclusion of the day's fighting, only 99 men regrouped.

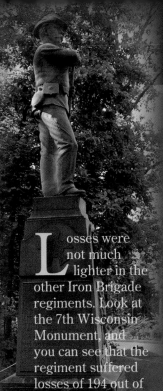

Regimental Markers

osses were not much lighter in the other Iron Brigade regiments. Look at the 7th Wisconsin Monument, and you can see that the regiment suffered losses of 194 out of 370 present for duty on July 1. You'll also see that the 7th Wisconsin suffered a total of 1,157 casualties throughout the war.

The Iron Brigade relieved Buford's cavalry fighting south of the Chambersburg Pike during the morning of July 1. After repulsing the attack of Archer's Brigade of Heth's Division, the regiment fought on McPherson's Ridge before being pushed back to Seminary Ridge in the afternoon.

Day I visited

Who I was with

The first thing I noticed was

The Iron Brigade is famous because

One reason so many died might be

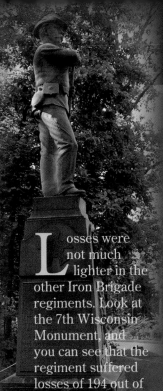

STAMPS

Don't forget to write your friends and family back home.

POSTCARDS

Names	Addresses

Collect brochures
from all the
interesting places
you visit.

Brochures

John Reynolds

Day I visited

Who I was with

The first thing I noticed was

The most interesting thing I learned about

General John Reynolds was

One thing I will always remember is

As you finish your drive circuit around Meredith Drive, you come back to Reynolds Avenue on McPherson's Ridge. If you look off to the left you see a stone pillar that marks the spot where Union General John Reynolds was shot and killed during the early action of July 1. Reynolds was hit in the head as he rode along the front lines encouraging the Iron Brigade. Reynolds' death is sometimes attributed to a Confederate sniper, but the most likely cause was a bullet fired by a Confederate infantryman of Archer's Brigade. The general died instantly.

As you approach Chambersburg Pike along Reynolds Avenue again, look off to your left at the barn on the opposite ridge. The barn occupies the spot of McPherson's Barn. This barn was used as a hospital by the Confederate Army during the battle. Imagine what it was like to be a Union cavalryman or infantryman crouching behind a barricade of fence rails as the Confederate infantry crested the ridge opposite to you and advanced across the shallow valley in front of you. During the fighting the valley would have been blanketed with smoke from the black-powder rifled muskets and carbines used by both armies.

Date I visited

Who I was with

The first thing I noticed was

Fighting a battle in this area would have been

The most interesting thing I learned was

Willoughby Run

Day I visited

Who I was with

The first thing I noticed was

The tremendous loss of life made me feel

One thing I'll always remember is

Stop at the Archer's Brigade monument right after the turn on Meredith Avenue past the three Iron Brigade regimental monuments, and you will see a small dirt path leading down to the creek called Willoughby Run. As you come out to the stream you will see that it isn't very wide. This is the place where the 26th North Carolina Infantry attacked on July 1. In crossing this short distance, five color bearers (the men who carried the regimental flag) were shot. The regiment suffered 588 casualties out of 800 present for duty on July 1. The regiment also took part in Pickett's Charge on July 3, after which only 90 men were left. The regiment's total loss of 88% during the battle was the highest percentage loss of any unit, Union or Confederate, during the Battle of Gettysburg.

Railroad Cut

After you cross the Chambersburg Pike you come to a small bridge over a railroad track. This railroad cut was the scene of fierce fighting on July 1. Cutler's Brigade of Union infantry held McPherson's Ridge on either side of this cut, which was unfinished at the time of the battle. Under attack from Davis' Brigade of Confederate infantry, the Union forces abandoned the line to the north of the cut. Elements of the 2nd and 42nd Mississippi and 55th North Carolina Infantry poured into the cut and began to push south, where they were met by the 6th Wisconsin Infantry, which had been detached from the Iron Brigade. After stopping the Confederate advance, the 6th Wisconsin and 95th New York attacked and pushed the Confederates back into the railroad cut.

Day I visited

Who I was with

The first thing I noticed was

Thinking about the fierce battle here made me fee

An important thing I learned was

Union & Confederate Officers

Across

3. To go after wildlife is to
5. Sounds like the color of the "go" signal
6. A covering for the head
8. In Communist countries there are many hammers and
9. President Harding's first name was his last name
10. Revolutionary War hero was known as "Lighthorse" Harry
12. A small mountain is a
13. "Inventor" of baseball

Down

1. Same name as a line of English kings
2. Spelled closely to a kind of fence
3. Last name in common with a signer of the Declaration of Independence
4. Wrestler Dusty _____
7. Popular tin foil
11. The opposite of late is

The 6th Wisconsin and 95th New York pushed up to the edge of the railroad cut, where you can see the flank markers of each regiment. The 6th Wisconsin then turned left and began to fire along the length of the cut where the men of Davis' brigade were now trapped. A charge by the 6th Wisconsin that was led by Colonel Dawes' who shouted "Align on the colors!" caused Confederate resistance to collapse. Hundreds of Mississippi and North Carolina soldiers surrendered.

Day I visited

Who I was with

The first thing I noticed was

I saw flank markers for

One reason I think the soldiers surrendered was

Day I visited

Who I was with

The first thing I noticed was

This monument taught me

Thinking about the battle here makes me feel

The triumph of the men from Wisconsin and New York was short-lived. By midafternoon Confederate attacks forced all Union forces off McPherson's Ridge, to Seminary Ridge, and finally to Culp's Hill and Cemetery Hill south of Gettysburg.

If you look beyond the regimental monument to the 84th New York (also known as the 14th Brooklyn) you can see McPherson's Barn and the Chambersburg Pike. The monument to the 6th Wisconsin lists the casualties during the battle, and during the entire war.

147th NY Infantry

This unit was one of Curtis' three infantry regiments that were initially deployed north of the railroad cut. When Davis' Brigade attacked those three units, the 84th New York and 95th New York received the order to withdraw south of the cut, but the 147th did not. The commander of the 147th, Lieutenant Colonel Miller, was wounded just as he received the order to withdraw. As Davis' Brigade took possession of the cut, the 147th was cut off from the rest of the Union army. Led by Major Harney, the regiment fought on, surrounded, until the attack of the 6th Wisconsin and 95th New York pushed the Confederate forces back. In a half-hour's fighting the 147th New York lost 301 out of 380 men.

Day I visited

Who I was with

The first thing that I noticed was

This monument taught me

I will always remember

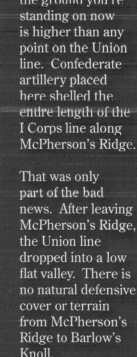

The two photographs on this page give you an idea of the terrain that was crucial to the Confederate success on the afternoon of July 1. The top photograph was taken from the Eternal Peace Memorial. McPherson's Ridge is on the left of the photo, and you can see how the ground you're standing on now is higher than any point on the Union line. Confederate artillery placed here shelled the entire length of the I Corps line along McPherson's Ridge.

That was only part of the bad news. After leaving McPherson's Ridge, the Union line dropped into a low flat valley. There is no natural defensive cover or terrain from McPherson's Ridge to Barlow's Knoll.

Day I visited

Who I was with

The first thing I noticed was

One thing that made this battle so difficult was

Eternal Peace Memorial

T he Eternal Peace Memorial crowns Oak Hill where Rodes' Division of Confederate infantry massed on July 1. The memorial was dedicated on July 3, 1938 at the 75th anniversary of the Battle of Gettysburg. All surviving veterans of the battle, Union and Confederate, were invited to attend, with their traveling expenses paid by the federal government. Almost 2000 made the trip, and formed part of the crowd of 200,000 that gathered to hear President Franklin D. Roosevelt dedicate this monument. The monument is made from Alabama limestone and Maine granite. Its message of peace is summed up in the inscription across the base of the monument, "Peace Eternal In A Nation United."

Day I visited

Who I was with

The first thing I noticed was

This memorial is important because

One thing I learned was

Cannons

Day I visited

Who I was with

One interesting fact I learned was

I think the howitzer shot weighed

A short stroll to the left of the Memorial brings you to two artillery pieces similar to those used in the fighting. The cannon with a greenish barrel is a 12-pound howitzer. The howitzer could fire a solid shot (guess how much it weighed?), a shell, or canister. The cannon with a black barrel and the screw on the end is a Whitworth 2.75 inch rifle. The rifling in the barrel caused the shell to rotate around an axis which made the cannon more accurate than the howitzer, which was a smoothbore. The other difference between the two is that the brass howitzer is a muzzle-loader, and the Whitworth rifle is a breechloader. These two pieces represent the end of an era of muzzle-loading smoothbore cannon, and the beginning of the era of breech-loading rifled cannon.

There is an observation tower here from which you have a good view of the northern end of the battlefield. There are also a number of regimental monuments that you can visit at your leisure. One of the more informative but less obvious monuments is the pair of flank markers of the 16th Maine Infantry, shown in the photograph. The 275 officers and enlisted men of the regiment filled the space between these two markers. This gives you some idea of how close together men were in the battle lines. Of the 275 who went into action, 11 were killed, 62 wounded, and 159 taken prisoner after being surrounded.

Day I visited

Who I was with

The first thing I noticed was

Some of the more interesting monuments were

One thing I learned here was

The tightness of the battle field made me wonder

Barlow's Knoll

Day I visited _____

Who I was with _____

_____

The first thing I noticed was _____

_____

_____

One interesting thing I saw was _____

Retreating was/was not good because _____

_____

_____

_____

_____

_____

_____

_____

If you climb the observation tower on Oak Ridge and look off to the east this is the view that you will have. The small rise in the middle of the photo with the flagpole rising from it is Barlow's Knoll, which was the right flank of the Union XI Corps. The 8,300 infantry of the XI Corps formed a line from Oak Ridge over to Barlow's Knoll. When the Confederate divisions of Rodes and Early attacked this position on the afternoon of July 1, the outnumbered and outflanked XI Corps was forced to retreat through the town of Gettysburg and re form on Cemetery Hill. During the retreat, the Battery I, 1st Ohio Light Artillery, commanded by Captain Hubert Dilger, dueled with Confederate artillery and infantry.

His Union division formed the right flank of the XI Corps line. The small hill was attacked by Doles' Brigade of Rodes' Division and Gordon's Brigade of Early's Division in the afternoon of July 1. The Union troops retreated, and General Barlow was severely wounded and captured during the retreat.

After being taken prisoner, General Barlow was tended by Confederate surgeons who gave him little chance to live. News was sent through the lines to Barlow's wife Arabella who was serving as a nurse with the Union Army that her husband was wounded. She arrived on July 4 to tend to him. Although he survived his wounds, sadly, she lived only one more year before dying of typhus contracted while serving in a Union hospital.

Day I visited

Who I was with

The first thing I noticed was

This site made me feel

An important fact I learned was

Adams County Almshouse

Day I visited

Who I was with

The first thing I noticed was

This oldest date I could find was

South of Barlow's Knoll you see a small cemetery. This was the burial ground for the Adams County Almshouse, or poorhouse, through most of the 19th and 20th centuries. You won't find any headstones predating the battle if you walk among the graves, but you will find some from the 1870's. The almshouse was south of this small burial plot. Barlow originally deployed the two brigades of his division by the almshouse, but then moved up to the knoll that now bears his name as it afforded better lines of sight and fire.

The massive domed monument on Cemetery Ridge is the Pennsylvania State Monument. Dedicated in 1910, it is adorned by a winged victory on the cupola. The Pennsylvania generals who fought at Gettysburg have their names inscribed around the top of the monument. The 34,530 enlisted men and officers from Pennsylvania have their names inscribed in brass tablets on the base of the monument, arranged by regiment. The regimental plaques are organized by companies, as shown in the photo on this page. A small star next to the name of a soldier indicates that he was killed or mortally wounded during the Battle of Gettysburg.

Day I visited

Who I was with

The first thing I noticed was

As I read the names I felt

Some names I recognized were

I will always remember

1st MN Infantry

Day I visited

Who I was with

The first thing I noticed was

Minnesota losing 82% of their troops

makes me think

One thing I will remember is

The monument on Cemetery Ridge memorializes the charge made on the afternoon of July 2nd. General Cadmus Wilcox's brigade of Alabama infantry was moving to attack Union positions on the southern end of Cemetery Ridge. The troops there were the 1st Minnesota Infantry. General Winfield Hancock ordered the lone Minnesota regiment to attack the advancing Confederate brigade. They charged and stopped the advancing Alabamians. Wilcox's men quickly deployed and exchanged volleys with the 1st Minnesota. After fifteen minutes, more Union troops came up to plug the gap on the southern end of Cemetery Ridge, and the 1st Minnesota withdrew. 262 men had made that desperate charge, and only 47 returned, for a loss of 82%.

The drive along Seminary Ridge is marked by several state monuments for the Confederate units that fought at Gettysburg. The North Carolina State Monument, dedicated in 1929, features a sculptural group consisting of four figures. The kneeling figure is an officer pointing the way forward to his troops. There are two standing infantrymen, followed by a color bearer. All of the figures have faces modeled using photographs of Confederate soldiers. The color bearer is modeled on the face of Orren Randolph Smith, a native of North Carolina whom many say designed the Stars and Bars, the Confederate flag, in March 1861. Over a quarter of the casualties that the Army of Northern Virginia suffered at Gettysburg were North Carolinians.

Day I visited

Who I was with

The first thing I noticed was

The faces on the sculpture seemed

The most interesting thing I learned was

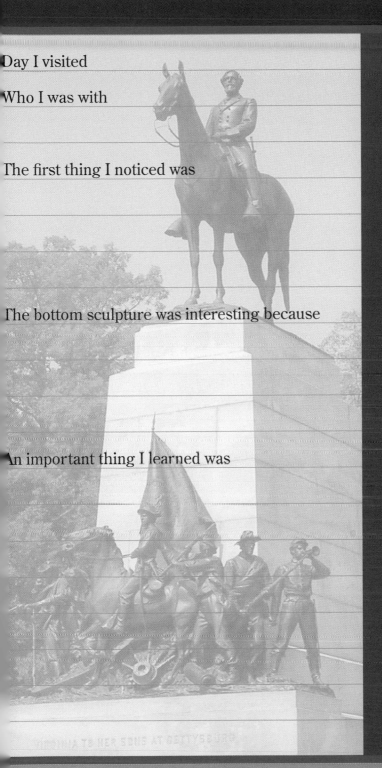

Day I visited

Who I was with

The first thing I noticed was

The bottom sculpture was interesting because

An important thing I learned was

VIRGINIA TO HER SONS AT GETTYSBURG

The Virginia State Monument was the first Confederate monument to be erected on the battlefield. In 1917 this memorial, consisting of an equestrian statue of General Robert E. Lee and a sculptural group of seven Virginia soldiers, was placed at the vantage point from which Lee observed some of the action on July 2 and 3. The sculptor, Frederick W. Sievers, worked from masks and photographs of Lee, as well as from the preserved skeleton of Traveller, Lee's horse. The seven figures at the base consist of two boys, the bugler and cavalry color bearer, as well as a professional man, a businessman, a mechanic, a farmer, and an artist, representing men from all walks of life. The battlefield debris in which they stand reminds us of the sacrifices that they made.

South of the North Carolina Memorial stands the Tennessee State Memorial, the last State Memorial to be erected on the battlefield. The three stars on the top of the stone slab represent the 1st, 7th, and 14th Tennessee Infantry regiments, as do the three figures etched into the slab. The base is 16 feet long, commemorating the fact that Tennessee was the 16th state to enter the Union. The vertical slab rests on a stone outline of the state itself. On the back face of the monument the losses (396 out of 775 present) of the regiments are listed. These three regiments served in Heth's Division of Hill's Corps, and were involved in the heavy fighting of July 1 on McPherson's and Seminary Ridge, as well as the climactic assault known as Pickett's Charge on July 3.

Day I visited

Who I was with

The first thing I noticed was

This memorial taught me that

Day I visited

Who I was with

The first thing I noticed was

The three stars represented the

As you drive further south along Seminary Ridge you see a number of state monuments erected by the states of the former Confederacy. The Florida State Memorial commemorates the participation of the 2nd, 5th, and 8th Florida Infantry in the battle. These three regiments, comprising the smallest Confederate brigade to serve at Gettysburg, are symbolized by the three stars on the vertical stone bearing the inscription. The losses, 445 out of 700, were proportionally the heaviest of any Confederate brigade. The memorial was dedicated here on July 3, 1963, on the 100th anniversary of the battle. Perry's Brigade, which was actually commanded by Colonel David Lang, participated in the assault on the Union left on July 2, and the assault on the Union center on July 3.

Before you come to the memorials of Louisiana and Mississippi by the Pitzer farm, there is a turnoff to the right that leads to a small cul-de-sac. You see three monuments here, two of which are shown on this page. The short square stone plinth commemorates the 3rd Maine Infantry, and the other two monuments commemorate companies of Berdan's Sharpshooters. These units performed a reconnaissance in the early afternoon of July 2, probing the Confederate positions near the Spangler and Pitzer farms. They ran into elements of Wilcox's Brigade, and after skirmishing with the Alabamians the 3rd Maine and four companies of the Sharpshooters retreated back to the Peach Orchard.

Day I visited

Who I was with

The first thing I noticed was

One thing I learned was

3RD MAINE INFANTRY ENGAGED HERE FORENOON OF JULY 2ND 1863.

Sharpshooter Differences

Day I visited

Who I was with

The first thing I noticed was

Sharpshooting seems

One interesting fact I learned here was

The difference between Berdan's Sharpshooters and the standard infantry sharpshooter may be seen in these two monuments on Cemetery Ridge. The two regiments of Berdan's sharpshooters were formed from companies raised individually from the states. They were armed with breech-loading rifles which they could fire twice as fast as the usual muzzleloading muskets. The usual equipment is shown in the monument to the Massachusetts sharpshooters. Their sniper rifles weighed approximately thirty pounds and had a telescopic sight. These cumbersome rifles were usually fired from a rest, such as a fence rail or tree limb. While these sniper rifles were accurate at long ranges, they were difficult to fire quickly.

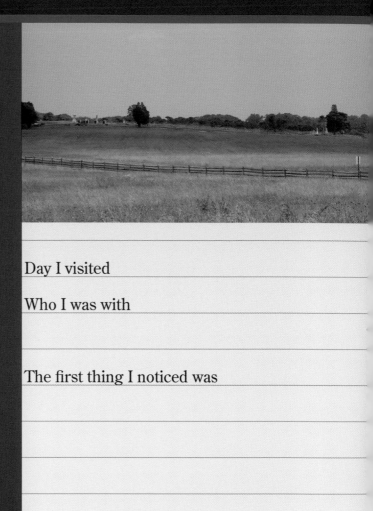

If you walk out to the edge of the Pitzer farm and look east you will see the Peach Orchard. This small rise gives good fields of fire and lines of sight all around to whichever side occupied it. In the early afternoon of July 2, General Dan Sickles, commanding the Union III Corps, moved his troops from the southern end of Cemetery Ridge up to this position. This advance put his corps over half a mile out in front of the rest of the Union Army. General James Longstreet, commanding the assault on the Union left, placed 54 artillery pieces so that their fire converged on this salient in the Union line. The Confederate assault on the Union Corps began around 4, and struck the Peach Orchard at about 5:30. Led by Barksdale's Mississippi Brigade, the Confederate attack crumpled up the Union defensive position.

Day I visited

Who I was with

The first thing I noticed was

This is a good battlesite because

AL State Monument

Day I visited _____

Who I was with _____

_____

The first thing I noticed was _____

One interesting thing about

this statue is _____

The Alabama State Monument marks the approximate position of General Evander Law's Brigade (4th, 15th, 44th, 47th, 48th Alabama Infantry Regiments) of General John B. Hood's Division. The female figure represents The Spirit of Alabama. She is flanked on her left by a soldier representing Spirit and on her right by a soldier representing Determination. While she comforts the figure on the left she points the way forward to the figure on the right.

Law's Brigade formed the right flank unit of the Confederate assault on the Union left. After smashing through the Union lines around Devil's Den, it swept toward Little Round Top. If Law's men could hold that small hill, the Union army's position would be in grave danger.

Devil's Den

While the mass of large granite boulders and broken ground are fun to climb on and explore today, Devil's Den was a difficult place to fight a battle. The left end of the Union III Corps was anchored here by General J.H. Hobart Ward's Brigade of Birney's Division. The Confederate attack of Law's Alabama Brigade, supported by the Texas Brigade commanded by General J.B. Robertson, routed the Union forces here. Both Confederate brigades were soon driving on toward Little Round Top, which you can just see in the distance beyond the rocks in Devil's Den.

Day I visited

Who I was with

The first thing I noticed was

Climbing the rocks showed me

One thing I will always remember is

Little Round Top

Day I visited _____

Who I was with _____

_____

The first thing I noticed was _____

_____

One thing I found interesting was _____

_____

_____

_____

_____

_____

_____

_____

As the four Confederate brigades of Hood's Division were smashing through the Birney's Division of the III Corps, General G.K. Warren found only a small signal detachment on Little Round Top. On this page you have a view north from along the Union line on Cemetery Ridge, and you can see that if the Confederates had positioned artillery up here, they could fire along the length of the Union line. Warren, who was the chief engineer on General Meade's staff, immediately sent a messenger to General George Sykes, who was bringing his V Corps up to reinforce the shattered units of Sickles' III Corps. Two Union brigades ascended the north side of Little Round Top as men from Robertson's and Law's brigades were coming up the south side.

The men of Vincent's brigade won the race for the hill. Colonel Vincent deployed his four regiments with the 20th Maine on the left.

The Union men fought from behind piled-up fence rails and rocks, repulsing several attacks by the men of Alabama and Texas. The 20th Maine was particularly vulnerable. After repelling several attacks, Colonel Joshua Chamberlain of the 20th Maine led his men in a desperate bayonet charge that drove the Confederates back for good, and Little Round Top was saved.

If you look at the monument of the 20th Maine, you see that the losses in the regiment are listed by company. Every company except company B is listed. Why was that company left off?

Day I visited

Who I was with

The first thing I noticed was

There were less trees back then so the battle was

Company B was left off because

TWENTIETH MAINE

Day I visited _____

Who I was with _____

_____

_____

The first thing I noticed was _____

_____

_____

This monument seemed _____

_____

_____

The spiral staircase led me to _____

Too often when the story of the defense of Little Round Top is told, only the exploits of the 20th Maine are mentioned. At the summit of this hill you'll find the monument commemorating the 44th New York, the 140th New York, commanded by Colonel Patrick O'Rourke (could his name have been more Irish?).

The 44th New York Infantry regimental monument is the largest on the battlefield, standing 44 feet high. Two companies of the 12th New York also served with the 44th at Little Round Top, which is why the lower room of this castle is twelve feet square.

The small monument to the 140th New York infantry marks the spot where Colonel O'Rourke was killed as his regiment charged.

The Irish theme continues at three of the monuments that you pass while traveling along Sickles Avenue on the way to the Wheatfield. The first monument is a large Celtic cross that commemorates the Irish Brigade regiments of the 63rd, 69th, and 88th New York. The large harp, and the life-size bronze Irish wolfhound at the base of the cross makes the Irish association plain. The Irish brigade also contained the 28th Massachusetts and the 116th Pennsylvania. The monument to the 28th Massachusetts is a little further along, and carries the inscription "Faugh A Ballaugh." This Gaelic war cry means "Clear the Way." The Irish Brigade was so under strength at Gettysburg that all five regiments combined had only 530 men, a testament to the hard fighting of the brigade.

Day I visited

Who I was with

The first thing I noticed was

These monuments were interesting because

One thing I learned here was

Day I visited

Who I was with

The first thing I noticed was

These monuments are dedicated to

As you climb the small hill by the Irish Brigade monuments you come out to the Wheatfield. This 19-acre field of wheat was the scene of intense close-range fighting for four hours on the afternoon of July 2. The assault on the Union position here was launched by Anderson's Brigade of Hood's Division against DeTrobni-and's Brigade. Both sides poured reinforcements into this cauldron of fighting. Charge and counter-charge swept back and forth across the field with neither side gaining an advantage. When Union forces pulled back toward Cemetery Ridge, over 4,000 men lay here wounded or dead as the sun went down, along with General Semmes, a Confederate brigade commander, and General Zook, a Union brigade commander.

As you proceed north you come to Sickles Avenue off to the right. The monument with five columns commemorates the Excelsior Brigade (70th, 71st, 72nd, 73rd, 74th New York Infantry). Past the columned monument you see another commemorating the 2nd Fire Zouaves, a regiment that became the 73rd New York Infantry. The "Fire" part of their name derives from the regiment being composed mostly of New York volunteer firemen. The "Zouaves" part of their name derives from uniforms modeled on the French Zouaves who fought in North Africa, and often consisted of baggy bright red trousers and short tight blue jackets. These fancy uniforms were discarded in 1862, and the Union Zouave regiments wore the regulation blue uniform.

Day I visted

Who I was with

The first thing I noticed was

These monuments taught me

Continuing on Sickles Avenue and making a right brings you to a cluster of farm buildings. This is the Trostle Farm. On the right side of the road you see a marker indicating the position of General Sickles' headquarters on July 2. Sickles was severely wounded here by a cannon ball, and his right leg was amputated. Today you can see the actual amputated leg in the National Museum of Health and Medicine in Washington, D.C.

As the Union lines along the Wheatfield and Peach Orchard collapsed, the Union artillery covered the retreat. The 9th Massachusetts Artillery fought off Barksdale's Brigade, until the 21st Mississippi overran the battery in a fury of hand-to-hand fighting among the six guns. The victorious Confederates then charged on towards Cemetery Ridge.

Day I visited

Who I was with

The first thing I noticed was

think fighting a battle here would have been

As the men of Barksdale's and Wofford's Brigades advanced past the Trostle Farm, they were met by a line of 24 cannons from the Artillery Reserve commanded by Lieutenant Colonel McGilvery. The infantry of the 21st Mississippi were able to follow the survivors of Bigelow's 9th Massachusetts Artillery into the gun line, where they overran Battery I of the 5th US Artillery. The other three batteries never let up firing the scorching volleys of canister into the Plum Run valley, and the 39th New York Infantry soon drove the few Mississippians who had charged the gun line back toward the Trostle Farm. As you stand behind the cannon, you can get an idea of the view a Union artilleryman had of the Trostle Farm from McGilvery's massed batteries.

Day I visited

Who I was with

The first thing I noticed was

Cannons were important in battle because

One interesting thing I learned here was

Day I visited

Who I was with

The first thing I noticed was

The memorial here taught me

While The Confederate First Corps under Longstreet was attacking the left end of the Union line, the right end was assailed by the Second Corps under Ewell. General Ewell ordered Latimer's Artillery Battalion to prepare the way for an infantry assault. Latimer's 14 guns fought a 90-minute artillery duel with 24 Federal guns on Cemetery Hill. The Federal artillery suppressed the Confederate fire, and mortally wounded the 19-year-old Major Latimer in the process. General Ewell would have to send his infantry against the Union positions on Culp's Hill and Cemetery Hill without artillery support.

MAD LIB

MAD LIB

Before loooking at the story below, write in what words come to mind in the columns below. Then fill in the blank spaces with the words you have picked according to the number.

1. Adjective _____
2. Person's Name _____
3. Verb _____
4. Plural Noun _____
5. Verb ending in "ing" _____
6. Person's Name _____
7. Verb _____
8. Adverb _____
9. Adjective _____
10. Exclamation _____
11. Verb _____
12. Adjective _____

13. Plural Noun _____
14. Adjective _____
15. Plural Noun _____
16. Occupation ending in "ing" _____
17. Noun _____
18. Person's Name _____
19. Adjective _____
20. Noun _____
21. Verb in Past Tense _____
22. Adverb _____
23. Verb ending in "ing" _____
24. Plural Noun _____

Dear Diary,

Ever since I arrived I've been feeling pretty 1._____. 2._____ said I'd better 3._____ fast or I would miss seeing 4._____ at the site. So as soon as I finished 5._____ breakfast, I asked 6._____ to 7._____ ____ the car so we could get an early start. Once we arrived I couldn't wait to 8._____ look at the 9._____ battle sites. The first cannon I saw made me say 10._____ and I thought I would 11._____. The weapons from back then were really 12._____ _____ and they must have been made with 13._____. I think 14._____ 15._____ would be an interesting combination to use as a weapon. Maybe in the future I will study 16._____ so I can become a professional 17._____ builder. 18. _____ said, "Look! There's a 19._____ 20._____." I 21._____ _____ to it, but by the time I got there, it was 22._____ 23._____. Oh well, next time I need to pay more attention to 24._____ so I don't miss anything.

my trip to Gettysburg

Day I visited

Who I was with

The first thing I noticed was

The monument taught me

One new thing I learned is

After the artillery duel around the northern part of the Union line on the afternoon of July 2, Johnson's Division of Ewell's Corps began their assault on Culp's Hill. Back then, most of the brush and small trees you see today had been cleared which gave the Union defenders excellent fields of fire. Only a single brigade of 1,400 men was in the breastworks to meet the assault as most of Slocum's XII Corps had been shifted to the Union left to reinforce the crumbling Union lines there. The Confederates attacked from 8 pm for several hours, then resumed their assaults the next day. This monument is to the 66th Ohio Infantry, which made a bayonet charge on Culp's Hill similar to that of the 20th Maine on Little Round Top on July 2.

The Civil War is sometimes called the war where brothers fought brothers. One monument you see here is to the 1st Maryland, Eastern Shore, Infantry. This Union regiment fought opposite the 1st Maryland Battalion Infantry in Steuart's Brigade of Johnson's Division on July 3. The other monument you see is to the 78th and 102nd New York Infantry. The monuments portray the Union soldiers firing at the confederates from behind piles of rocks and logs. These breastworks gave excellent protection against the Confederate rifle fire.

One of the Confederate soldiers killed here was Wesley Culp, a private in the 2nd Virginia Infantry. He had gown up in Gettysburg, but moved to Virginia in 1858. He enlisted in the 2nd Virginia in 1861.

Day I visited

Who I was with

The first thing I noticed was

My favorite monument was

One thing I learned here was

Col. Isaac Avery

Day I visited

Who I was with

The cannons made me feel

In the twilight of July 2 two brigades from General Jubal Early's division of Ewell's Corps attacked the Union positions on Cemetery Hill. Hays' Brigade and Hoke's Brigade led by Colonel Isaac Avery attacked elements of the Union XI Corps. The Union infantry could not hold back the charging Confederate infantry. The Confederate infantry stormed the artillery positions on the crest of the hill, until a counterattack by Carroll's Brigade of the Union II Corps drove them off. Colonel Avery fell mortally wounded in the fighting.

While there was an Indiana State Memorial on the battlefield as early as 1885, the present memorial dates from 1971. It marks the spot where on the morning of July 3 the 2nd Massachusetts and 27th Indiana Infantry were ordered to attack the Confederate positions at the base of Culp's Hill. These two regiments came under fire from two Confederate brigades and were shot to pieces as they advanced.

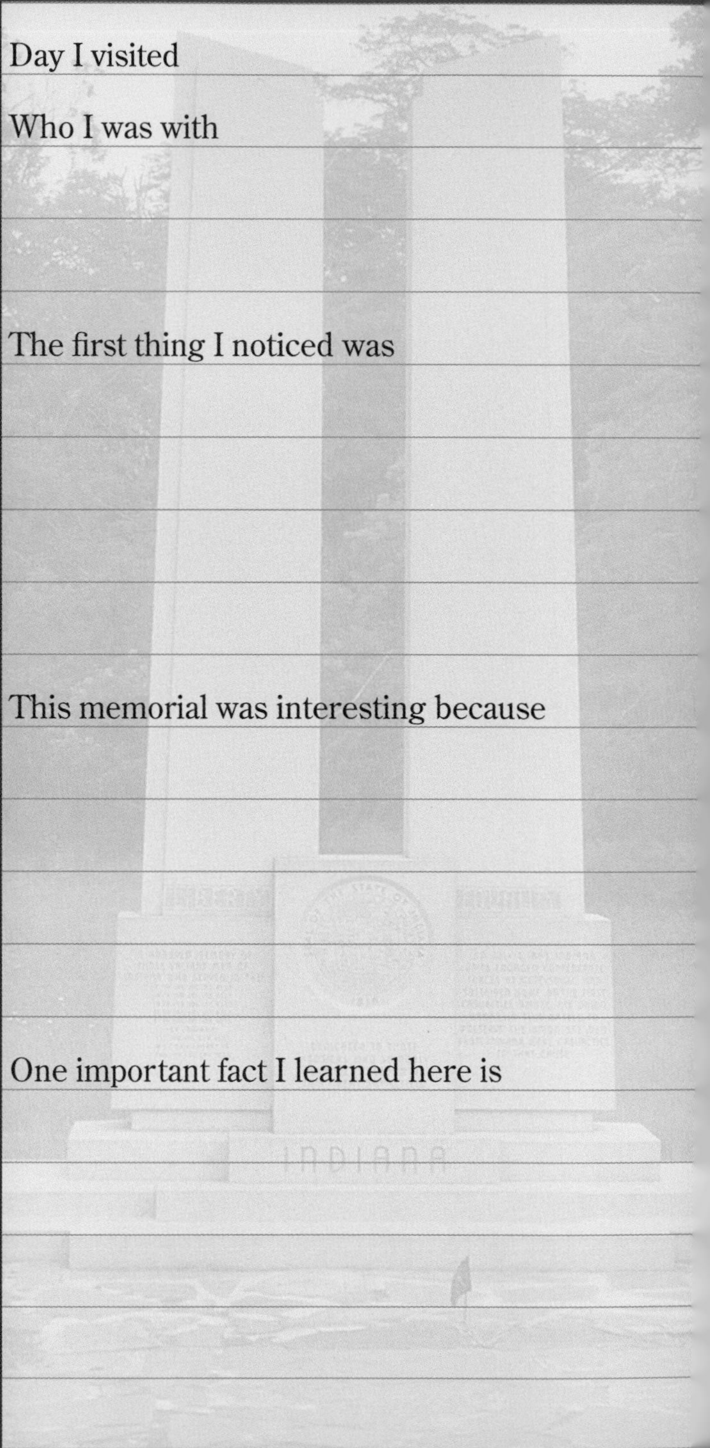

Day I visited

Who I was with

The first thing I noticed was

This memorial was interesting because

One important fact I learned here is

Day I visited

Who I was with

The first thing I noticed was

I know this is a cavalry monument because

Three miles east of Gettysburg the major cavalry action of the battle took place on July 3. The Cavalry Battlefield is worth a visit, particularly when the battlefield is crowded.

The Confederate cavalry was absent for the first two days of the battle. Lee planned to have Stuart take his cavalry and strike the Federal rear as Pickett's Charge hit the Union center on July 3. But Stuart's troopers were intercepted by Gregg's Division supported by a brigade of Michigan cavalry led by a young brigadier by the name of George Custer. The photograph shows the Runnel farm off to the right, and the high ground where Stuart deployed his cavalry around noon on July 3.

As you go further along the loop through the cavalry battlefield you will see a tall monument commemorating the action of Custer's Brigade. The 1st Michigan was led by General Custer in a countercharge against an assault column comprised of Fitz Lee's Brigade. Stuart was unable to drive the Union cavalry from the field, and so the back door to the Union rear remained closed.

Look at the plaques on the monument. There you see the names of Custer and Stuart, two of the most well-known American cavalry commanders of all time. You can also see that while the fighting may have been fiercely contested, the casualties suffered by Custer's Brigade were light compared to the losses suffered by many infantry units at Gettysburg.

Day I visited

Who I was with

The first thing I noticed was

From this monument I learned

One reason Custer's Brigade did better was

Cemetery Ridge

Day I visited

Who I was with

The first thing I noticed was

Cemetery Ridge is important because

If you stand on Seminary Ridge close to the North Carolina and Tennessee State Memorials and look to the east, you see the long low slope of Cemetery Ridge. The flank attacks that the Army of Northern Virginia had launched had nearly broken the Union position many times. Each time the Confederate victory was near, the Federal forces had managed to hang on and repulse the last assaults.

Lee planned to strike the center of the Union line on July 3. After some discussion with James Longstreet, whom Lee referred to as "my old war horse", the decision was made to hit the center of the Federal position with three divisions. These three divisions would have to cross over 1,000 yards of open ground to reach the Federal line.

This is the view a Federal soldier would have had while looking west toward Seminary Ridge on the afternoon of July 3. The white dot that you see in the middle of the dark line of trees is the Virginia State Monument. The horizontal white line across the center of the photograph is the Emmitsburg Road. Now, as then, it is bordered by a rail fence that would impede the movement of the Confederate troops. The rail fence is under 300 yards away. At that range Union rifle fire and canister from the artillery would inflict heavy casualties on the advancing brigades.

At about 1 o'clock in the afternoon, 170 Confederate artillery pieces began the bombardment of Cemetery Ridge.

Day I visited

Who I was with

The first thing I noticed was

One important thing I learned here was

The Clump of Trees

Day I visited

Who I was with

The first thing I noticed was

This site is important because

This clump of trees was the aiming point for the assault. The Union infantry took cover behind a stone wall that you can see in the lower left of the photograph. You should note that the infantry was not posted on the crest of the ridge. During the Confederate bombardment many of the shells passed over the infantry and hit the crest of the ridge or sailed over it completely. The noise and blast of the Confederate guns and the rain of shells and solid shot must have been scary, but it did little damage to the Union infantry waiting for the Confederate assault. After over an hour of bombardment, the Confederate guns fell silent to allow the infantry to make their assault.

A s you approach the Clump of Trees from the car park along Cemetery Ridge you see a large bronze book flanked by two artillery pieces. The open pages list the Confederate regiments that took part in the assault and the Federal units involved in their repulse. The monument was designed by Colonel John Bachelder, Superintendent of Tablets and Legends, to commemorate the deepest point of penetration of Pickett's Charge into the Union position. This point goes by the name "The High Water Mark of the Confederacy," and marks the point from which the fortunes of the Confederacy would spiral downward into defeat. The monument was dedicated in 1892.

Day I visited

Who I was with

The first thing I noticed was

The monument is unique because

The Angle

Day I visited

Who I was with

The first thing I noticed was

This battle site is important because

One thing I learned here is

To the north of the High Water Mark you see the Angle, the place where the stone wall behind which the Union troops took cover, turned east up the slope of Cemetery Ridge. At the corner of the Angle stands the monument to the 71st Pennsylvania Infantry, which together with the 69th Pennsylvania bore the brunt of the Confederate assault directed at the Clump of Trees.

The 71st Pennsylvania was pushed out of their position along the Angle by men from the brigades of General Garnett and General Armistead, two of Pickett's Brigade commanders. Garnett was killed, and Armistead mortally wounded, as their Virginia troops stormed into the Union position.

Between the Angle and the Clump of Trees you see this small stone monument in the form of a scroll. This marks the spot where General L.A. Armistead fell mortally wounded. He had led his men forward from Seminary Ridge with his black hat raised on the point of his sword, across the long shallow valley to Cemetery Ridge. By the time his brigade reached the Federal position, hundreds of his men had been shot. Armistead led a few hundred survivors across the stone wall, shouting "Give them the cold steel, boys!". Fired on from three sides and without reinforcements, the Confederates could not maintain their foothold in the Union line.

Day I visited

Who I was with

The first thing I noticed was

The interesting thing about this monument is

One thing I learned here is

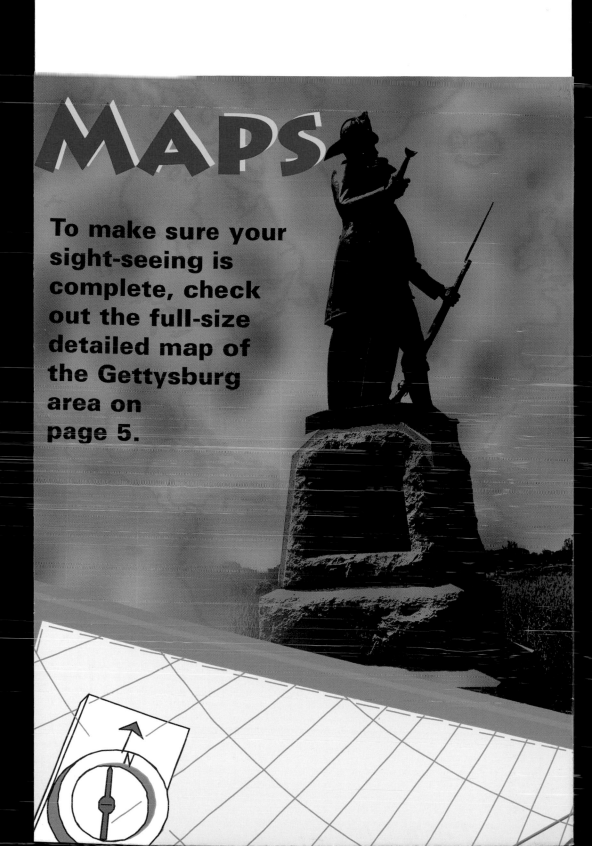

MAPS

To make sure your sight-seeing is complete, check out the full-size detailed map of the Gettysburg area on page 5.

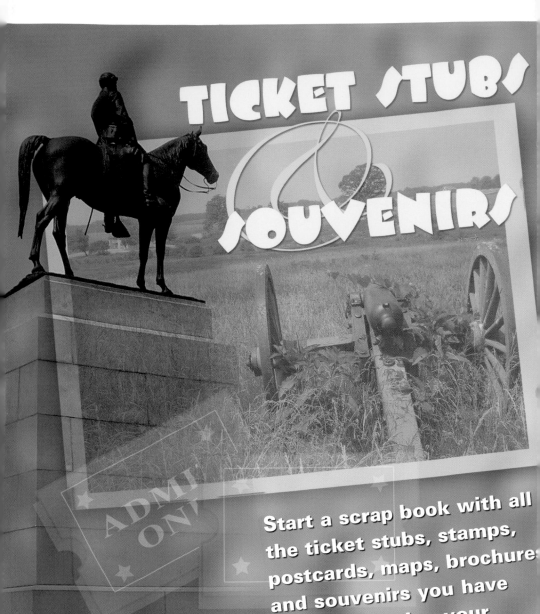

TICKET STUBS & SOUVENIRS

Start a scrap book with all the ticket stubs, stamps, postcards, maps, brochures and souvenirs you have collected during your exciting trip to Gettysburg. Share your scrap book with all your friends and famil

Word Search

```
D E D N U O R R U S S E O
T T R Y N I B E F A G C E
G A R R O I A R B D A I R
R R R E I E E E I V D A N
I E N T S G R R A G B I E
N D L E I F E L T T A B E
F E I M V L R A N R R D T
A F E E I Y L E R O R R E
N N E C D F M E L F I R K
T O Y B T U T N R N C N S
R C A N N O N T L Y A L U
Y N F O R C E S C A D D M
I I M U C A R B I N E A O
```

Word List:

ARTILLERY	CEMETERY	REGIMENT
BARRIGADE	CONFEDERATE	RIDGE
BATTLEFIELD	DIVISION	RIFLE
BRIGADE	FORGES	SABER
CANNON	MUSKET	TERRAIN
CARBINE	INFANTRY	UNION
CAVALRY	MONUMENT	

You need to walk south from the Clump of Trees, past the obelisk to find the marker that commemorates the spot where General Winfield Hancock was wounded during Pickett's Charge. The tall obelisk commemorates the service of the United States Regulars, with infantry, cavalry, artillery, and engineers being honored on each of its four faces.

Hancock was wounded at this spot as he ordered Stannard's Brigade forward to fire into the flanks of Pickett's assault column. A nail and wood splinters from his saddle were driven into his leg by enemy rifle fire. While he recovered and returned to command in 1864, recurring infection from his wound troubled him for the rest of his life.

Day I visited

Who I was with

The first thing I noticed was

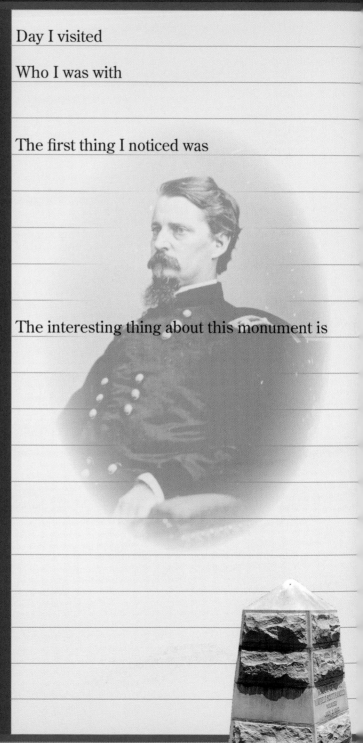

The interesting thing about this monument is

Gen. James Longstreet

Day I visited

Who I was with

The first thing I noticed was

I liked/disliked this sculpture because

One of the most recently erected monuments on the battlefield is the equestrian statue honoring General James Longstreet, commander of the First Corps, Army of Northern Virginia. This monument stands in the woods near the modern-day amphitheater, not far from the Louisiana State Monument. It was his corps that carried out the attacks on the Federal left on July 2, but his name will be forever associated with the great infantry assault on July 3. This attack, often known as Pickett's Charge, is more properly called Longstreet's Assault.

One of the more symbolic buildings on the battlefield is a group of farm buildings to the north of the Angle. The farm buildings of Abraham Brian, a free African-American farmer, stand here. The regimental monument of the 111th New York Infantry is also in the photograph. That the Confederacy would attain its High Water Mark on a ridge crowned by the farm of a free African-American family is deeply symbolic.

The Brian family vacated their farm at the end of June 1863 as the Confederate forces approached Gettysburg, as it was rumored that the Confederate armies would seize any African-Americans that they found and carry them off to the South and slavery.

Day I visited

Who I was with

The first thing I noticed was

This site is historically important because

Pickett's Charge

Day I visited

Who I was with

The first thing I noticed was

Pickett's Charge is very important because

A short asphalt path leads from the Virginia State Monument out towards Cemetery Ridge. One of the more poignant episodes of the battle took place here, where General Robert E. Lee met the remnants of the units that had taken part in Pickett's Charge. Lee rode out to meet his men and said to them, "It is my fault. It is all my fault." Rather than blame his men, Lee took full responsibility for the failure of the attack. Of the 12,500 men who made the attack, over 50% were casualties. In Pickett's Division all 15 regimental commanders were casualties, as were all three brigade commanders. Now when we look across this shallow valley we see a few trees and green fields. On July 3 1863 it was a smoking slaughterhouse.

The two most important commanders on the Union side are pictured here. The equestrian statue of General George Meade stands on Cemetery Ridge, across the road from The Angle and the Clump of Trees. The statue of Winfield Hancock stands on Cemetery Hill. Meade was elevated to command of the Army of the Potomac on June 27, just four days before the battle began. Meade showed no flashes of brilliance, but did fight the battle with a cool competence that enabled the Army of the Potomac to win. Hancock was the best combat commander on the Union side throughout the second and third day of the battle.

Day I visited

Who I was with

The first thing I noticed was

These monuments taught me

Gettysburg Cyclorama

Day I visited

Who I was with

The first thing I noticed was

From this painting I learned

Visitors to Gettysburg have the opportunity to visit one of the most impressive battle paintings in the world, the Gettysburg Cyclorama. This massive painting is hung in the Cyclorama building, close to the Soldiers' National Cemetery and the Visitors Center. The present dimensions of the painting are approximately 359 feet long and 27 feet high. Paul Philoppoteaux was commissioned to carry out this work, which he began in April 1882 with a visit to the battlefield. Philoppoteaux worked with a local photographer, William Tipton, who took a series of panoramic photographs from the top of a wooden tower that was erected east of The Angle on Cemetery Ridge.

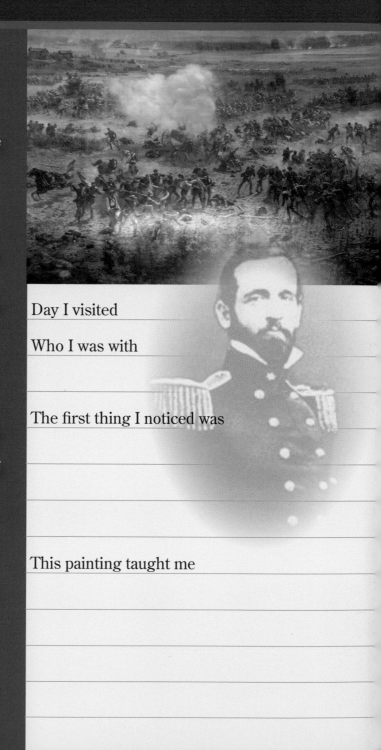

This section of the Cyclorama illustrates the death of General Richard Garnett, the second of Pickett's three brigade commanders to die at Gettysburg. Garnett is the mounted figure to the left of the top of the puff of smoke from the explosion in the middle of this scene.

The Cyclorama was first exhibited in Boston in 1884. The Cyclorama was exhibited in Philadelphia in 1891 and returned to Boston the following year. It was stored in a crate behind the exhibition hall under a small overhead roof. The painting deteriorated, and was bought in 1910 by Albert Hahne, who displayed sections of the Cyclorama in his department store in Newark, New Jersey.

Day I visited

Who I was with

The first thing I noticed was

This painting taught me

Gettysburg Cyclorama

Day I visited

Who I was with

The first thing I noticed was

The word "ahistorical" means

This detail of the section of the Cyclorama that depicts the repulse of Pettigrew's Division during Pickett's Charge shows another ahistorical entry in the painting. The Union officer with the drawn sword in the center of the painting who is leaning against a tree is a portrait of Paul Philoppoteaux, the artist who composed the Cyclorama. It was usual for an artist to insert himself, and his assistants, in a mammoth historical painting such as the Cyclorama.

In 1912 the Cyclorama was moved to Gettysburg, where it was exhibited in 1913 during the 50th anniversary of the battle. The painting was shown in a circular brick building on Cemetery Hill. The painting was moved to a new climate-controlled building in 1959 and underwent a thorough two-year restoration.

Lincoln Speech Memorial

Day I visited

Who I was with

The first thing I noticed was

This memorial is interesting because

One new thing I learned here is

The Lincoln Speech Memorial is on your right as you climb the hill from the Visitor's Center into the National Cemetery. The left bronze plaque commemorates the invitation extended to President Lincoln to come to Gettysburg for the dedication of the Soldiers' Cemetery. The right bronze plaque commemorates Lincoln's Gettysburg Address. The bundles of rods with an ax rising from the center of the bundle are fasces, ancient Roman symbols of the Roman Republic. This memorial is called the Lincoln Speech Memorial, but it does not sit on the spot where Lincoln gave his famous speech. This memorial was erected in 1912, but was never dedicated.

Soldiers' National Monument

Day I visited _____

Who I was with _____

The first thing I noticed was _____

This statue represents War _____

This statue represents History _____

This statue represents Plenty _____

This statue represents Peace _____

This was the first monument to be erected at Gettysburg. The dedication took place on July 1, 1869. The figure on the top of the central pillar represents Liberty. The four figures raised above the base represent War, History, Plenty, and Peace. (Can you figure out which statue represents which activity?) This memorial is sometimes incorrectly identified as the spot where Lincoln gave the Gettysburg Address.

The graves of the Federal dead from the battle are arranged by states. There are also 979 unknown Union soldiers buried here. The Confederate dead were not buried in this cemetery, but were exhumed after the war and returned to their respective states for burial there.

The Soldiers' National Cemetery is the resting place for soldiers from America's wars from the Civil War to the present. The majority of the graves are those of the Gettysburg dead, such as the Wisconsin plot containing 72 bodies, or one of the Unknown soldier plots with 425. But there are also war dead from other conflicts, like Seaman 1st Class George Stembosky, who died on December 7, 1941.

GEORGE
JOSEPH
STEMBROSKY

PENNSYLVANIA

S 1C US NAVY

WORLD WAR II

JANUARY 30 1921
DECEMBER 7 1941

Day I visited

Who I was with

The first thing I noticed was

I think Abraham Lincoln's words mean

As you look at all of the memorials, think on Lincoln's words, "The world will little note nor long remember what we say here, but it can never forget what they did here."

FRANCIS GERALD CORCORAN
M SGT
US ARMY
KOREA
VIETNAM
NOV 15 1928
DEC 9 1967

Dwight D. Eisenhower's Estate

Day I visited

Who I was with

The first thing I saw was

The neatest thing inside the house was

The most important thing I learned was

Before you leave Gettysburg, hop on the shuttle at the Visitor Center to visit the country estate of the 34th President of the United States, Dwight D. Eisenhower. He and his wife purchased this farm in 1950 and often used it as a weekend retreat, a place for dignitaries from around the world to meet, as well as their retirement home from 1961 – 1969. In 1967 the Eisenhowers deeded the property to the National Park Service. As you wander through the house, you will walk the same path of some of the greatest people in history, such as Soviet Primier Nikita Krushchev, Prime Minister Winston Churchill, and President Charles De Gaulle.

Sketch a monument

Use this page to sketch your favorite monument.